READING AND WRITING WORKSHOPS EDITION

NATIONAL GEOGRAPHIC Explorer!

CONTENTS

DEEP-SEA DIVER

Scientist Sylvia Earle shares her underwater adventures in this special interview.

Scuba gear lets Earle explore a coral reef covered with animals called soft coral.

Sylvia Earle peeks out from *DeepWorker*, the one-person submersible she uses to explore the sea.

NATALIE FOBES/ NATIONAL GEOGRAPHIC IMAGE COLLECTION

Oceans blanket 70 percent of our planet, yet we know more about the moon than the ocean. What plants and animals live in deep water? How do they survive the cold and the dark? And how are people affecting the health of the ocean (also called the sea)?

To look for answers, oceanographer Sylvia Earle is leading a series of underwater expeditions, or trips. She and other oceanographers use one-person submersibles, or underwater vessels, to explore the depths of the sea. Earle calls this five-year project the Sustainable Seas Expeditions. Between dives, she talked to NATIONAL GEOGRAPHIC EXPLORER about investigating the mysteries of the ocean.

Q. **How did you get started as an oceanographer?**

A. Earle: My family spent summer vacations along the New Jersey shore when I was a kid. A wave swept me off my feet at age three, and I fell in love with the sea. I was fascinated by the mysterious creatures at the ocean's edge: horseshoe crabs, sandpipers, even the tiny sand fleas! And I read everything I could find about the ocean. The more I learned, the more I wanted to know. I wondered what it would be like to swim with dolphins or to look a whale in the eye.

Q. What type of education does your work require?

A. Earle: It requires lots of science classes! Of course, for me, taking science classes was great fun. I studied marine biology at Florida State University and Duke University. My specialty was plants that live in the Gulf of Mexico.

Because I wanted to see plants and fish in their natural habitats, I also learned to scuba dive. I started when I was 17. Since then, I've spent about 6,000 hours underwater.

Q. How far down have you gone?

A. Earle: In 1991, I had the good luck to be a guest on *Shinkai 6500*, a Japanese submersible that holds three people. We went to 14,080 feet. That's about two and a half miles. We saw strange and wonderful things, including eels that shimmered like silver, tube-shaped animals called sea cucumbers, and a gorgeous fish with the awful name of "rat tail."

Q. Do you ever get scared down there?

A. Earle: Not very often. The sea feels much safer than crowded freeways or dark city streets! However, I do remember feeling nervous the first time I dived with humpback whales. It turned out I was right to be uneasy. I nearly bumped into one. She weighed 40-plus tons, and I thought I was history. But the whale swept by gracefully, missing me by inches.

Q. Tell us about the Sustainable Seas Expeditions.

A. Earle: Imagine moving into a house and never looking at three-quarters of the rooms! Pretty crazy, right? Well, we've never looked at most of our global home (the part that's water). So I'm working with a group of scientists to explore the ocean depths in areas off the coasts of California, Florida, Mexico, and the Central American country of Belize. We are looking at the fish and plants and comparing coral reefs in deep and shallow water.

The heart of each expedition is a submersible called *DeepWorker*. It is only eight feet long, five feet wide, and six feet high. That's just big enough to fit one person. *DeepWorker* can go 2,000 feet down, much deeper than a scuba diver.

All those arms help this cup coral snatch tiny animals to eat.

SYLVIA EARLE

The submersible has tools for taking pictures, shooting video, or recording sounds. It also has a special robotic arm that can pick up things. Best of all, the clear dome lets me or another oceanographer see whatever's going on. Piloting *DeepWorker* comes pretty close to my childhood dream of swimming with dolphins and whales.

Q. Why do we know so little about the ocean?

A. Earle: That's a good question. The main problem, I think, is that human beings don't have gills! We need special equipment—scuba gear, diving suits, or subs—just to breathe below the surface. Creating those high-tech tools takes time and money.

We also tend to take the ocean for granted. After all, it seems endless. We figure there are always more fish to catch, more places to dump trash. So we don't pause to ask how our actions affect the sea's health.

Q. What makes the sea so important?

A. Earle: The sea is basic to life itself. Plants in the sea provide most of our oxygen. And the water cycle, the journey of water from clouds to land and sea, then back to clouds, governs our climate. Subtract the ocean, and Earth would be another Mars—cold, harsh, empty. Does that sound like a place where you want to live?

Q. What's your advice for kids who want to explore the ocean?

A. Earle: Start exploring *today*. Even if you live hundreds of miles from the shore, get your feet wet by reading books about the sea. Find natural places near you and look at them with a scientist's eye. In other words, observe the plants and animals closely.

Look for patterns. Do sunny and shady places have different plants? Which animals are alone? Which seem to live in groups? Developing the habit of careful thinking will help in whatever you wind up doing.

As you get older, you can explore museum jobs, educational trips, and even college programs. There's no shortage of opportunity. The sea holds more mysteries than we can explore in my lifetime—or yours. And I can't think of a better place to work!

DeepWorker can travel 2,000 feet below the surface. The 8-foot-long sub is giving us new ways to look at our world.

6

Nuytco Rese

NEWTSUB
DeepWorker

KIP EVANS

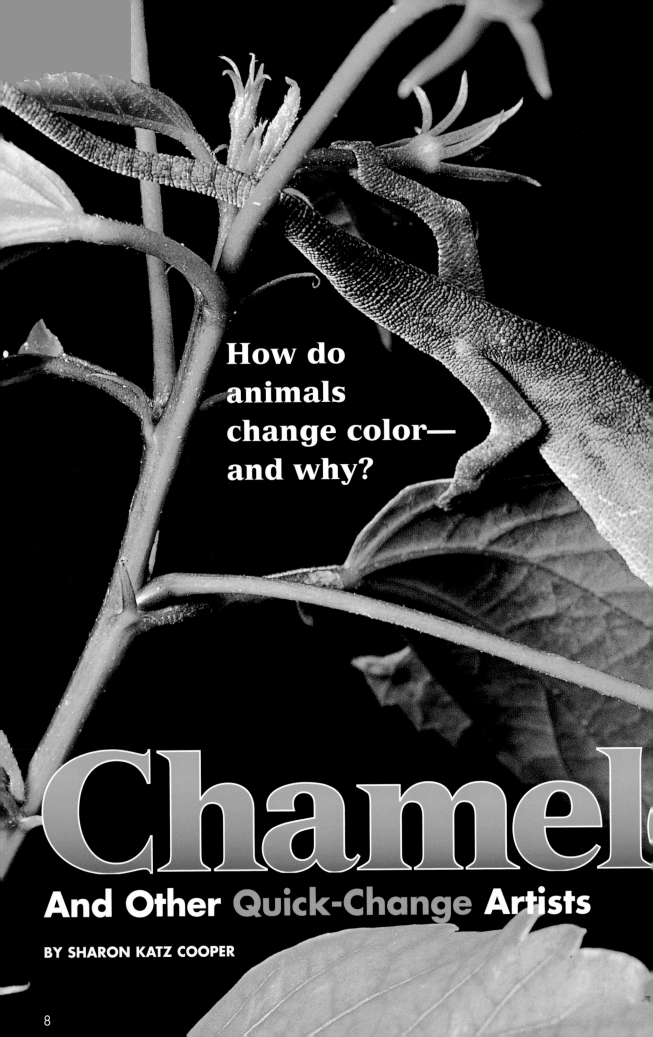

How do
animals
change color—
and why?

Chamel

And Other Quick-Change Artists

BY SHARON KATZ COOPER

What's green…then red…then yellow…then brown…then blue? A **chameleon.** This animal changes color often—and quickly. Sometimes you can even see it happen.

Changing Colors

Chameleons are born with special cells. These lie under the outer skin. The cells have a color, or **pigment,** in them. Some are red or yellow. Others are blue or white. The cells are called **chromatophores.**

Sometimes the brain sends a message. The message tells the chromatophores to get bigger or smaller. This causes the pigments to mix. It is a bit like mixing paint. When the pigments mix, the chameleon's skin color changes.

A chemical called **melanin** also helps chameleons turn color. Melanin can rise toward the skin's surface. This causes the skin to darken.

eons

Red With Rage. *Mood probably causes most color changes in chameleons. This creature is getting redder—and madder—by the moment!*

Why the Change?

Many people think chameleons change color to blend in. Scientists disagree. They say chameleons have other reasons to turn colors.

Changing color can make them more comfortable. If a chameleon is cold, it might turn darker. Why? Dark colors absorb more heat than light ones. This helps warm the chameleon.

In the sun, a chameleon might turn a lighter color. Light colors reflect bright sunlight. They keep the chameleon cool.

Changing color can also help chameleons communicate. A panther chameleon uses color to say that it is angry. This chameleon is normally green. When it gets angry, it turns red and yellow.

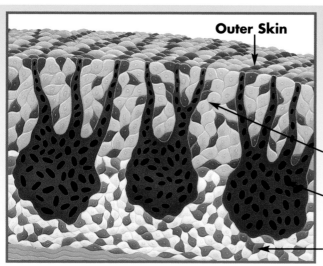

Outer Skin

Red and Yellow Cell Layers

Rising Melanin (red and black areas)

Blue and White Cell Layers

Color It Angry

Some color cells shrink and others expand to turn an angry chameleon's skin red and yellow. Also, a chemical called melanin rises toward the skin's surface. It causes areas in the skin to darken.

Camouflaged Critters

Chameleons are not the only creatures with chromatophores. Other animals have them too.

Many critters change color to keep from being seen. They use color to **camouflage,** or hide, themselves.

A golden tortoise beetle is usually bright gold. It can turn darker and spotted. This makes the beetle look like a ladybug. Many birds find beetles very tasty. But they don't like to eat ladybugs. So color helps the beetle hide from **predators.** These are animals that might eat it.

Predators change color too. A bark spider can turn brown, gray, green, or yellow. It blends in with trees, stones, and leaves. Then it waits for insects. Often the insects do not see the spider until it is too late. They become the spider's next snack!

Color Codes

Chameleons live in Africa, the Middle East, India, and Madagascar. Other quick-change artists live closer to home. Maybe someday you will watch one change color. Is the animal hot or cold? Hiding or showing off? Look carefully. Try to figure out its color code.

Yellow or White? *Two goldenrod spiders sit on flowers, waiting for prey. The spiders can camouflage themselves by changing colors—usually between yellow and white. Which spider above has a better chance of catching a tasty fly? Why?*

Wordwise

camouflage: to hide

chameleon: small– to medium–size lizard that has fancy crests, horns, or spines

chromatophores: skin cells that contain pigment

melanin: chemical that causes skin to darken

pigment: color found in cell

predator: animal that eats other animals

Melting A

Earth's temperature is rising. That is causing weather to change. It is also affecting wildlife.

By Glen Phelan

ray

Glacier National Park is in Montana. It is a beautiful park. It has towering cliffs. It has sharp ridges. It has deep valleys. All of these were made by ice.

Long ago, ice began to carve the rocks. Small pieces of ice could not do all that. But giant ice sheets could. They shaped the park's land.

Ice at Work

How do ice sheets form? Each winter, snow falls. Some of the snow melts in summer. But some stays. Year after year, this snow piles up. The mounds of snow get heavy. This makes the bottom layers of the mounds turn into ice. Then you have an ice sheet!

When an ice sheet gets heavy enough, it moves downhill. The ice sheet is now called a **glacier.**

Glacier National Park is named for its ice. Glaciers have shaped this land for millions of years. They push away soil. They carve valleys.

Glaciers are powerful. But they don't last forever. If the weather heats up, they melt. This happened thousands of years ago. Today, it is happening again.

© DAVID MUENCH, CORBIS

Warmer Waters. *Melting snow and ice formed this lake in Glacier National Park.*

I'm Melting

Many of the park's 26 glaciers are melting. Look at Grinnell Glacier. In 1910, it covered almost 440 acres of land. By 1931, it had shrunk to 290 acres. In 1998, it was only 180 acres. At this rate, Grinnell Glacier could soon melt away. So could the park's other glaciers.

Turning Up the Heat

Why is Grinnell Glacier melting? The park is heating up. It is about 3°F warmer than it was in 1910.

The rest of Earth is warming up too. This is called **global warming.** Since 1850, Earth has warmed about 1°F. Some places have warmed up more. Some have warmed up less.

Worldwide Warming

One degree may seem small. But it is causing big changes. It causes sea ice to melt. This is making life hard for animals that need the ice.

Global warming causes other problems too. For example, oceans are getting warmer. Some animals cannot survive in the warmer water.

DANIEL J. COX, NATURAL EXPOSURES

Snack Food. *A bear cub munches on springtime berries in a meadow in Glacier National Park.*

Causes for Warming

Why is Earth heating up? No one knows for sure. Some scientists blame **carbon dioxide.** That is a gas in the air. It traps heat. There is a lot of carbon dioxide in the air today. That might be why Earth is warmer.

Other scientists blame the sun. The sun's temperature can change. Some scientists think the sun is getting warmer. It may be sending more heat to Earth. This could be one reason why Earth is heating up.

The Meltdown

People do not know all the causes of global warming. But one thing is certain. Earth is warming up.

If this goes on, the whole planet could change. Lots of ice could melt. Rivers and oceans could rise and cause floods. Some plants and animals could become **extinct.** That means they could die out forever.

Glacier National Park would change too. Its glaciers would melt away. The park's plants and animals would be in trouble. Some would have to find new homes. Others could die out. Global warming could change life on every part of our planet.

 How is global warming changing the planet?

Wordwise

carbon dioxide: a gas in the air that traps heat

extinct: completely gone

glacier: ice that covers land and moves slowly downhill

global warming: worldwide rise in temperature

Arctic Sea Ice Coverage

Rising temperatures have affected the huge sheets of ice surrounding the North Pole. These images show how.

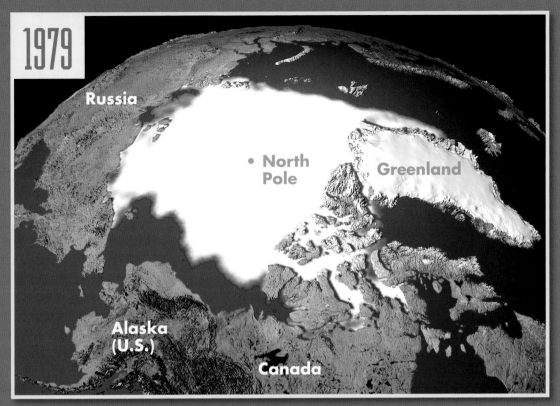

In 1979, ice covered much of the Arctic throughout the year.

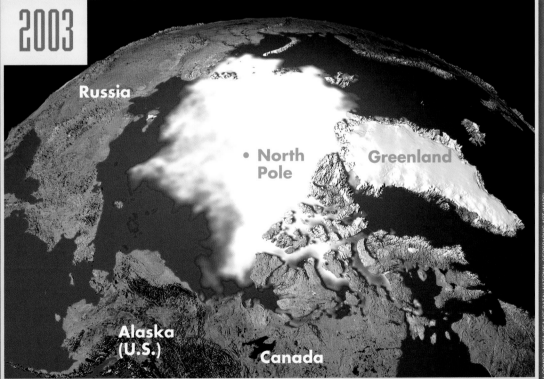

By 2003, large amounts of ice had melted. Where there was once solid ice, there is now ocean water. Many scientists say the ice in the area will continue to melt.

J. COMISO, NASA (SEA ICE DATA); NATIONAL GEOGRAPHIC ART (MAPS)

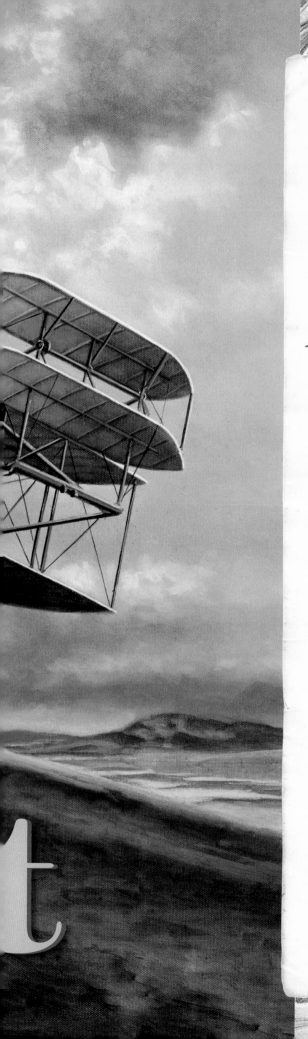

On December 17, 1903, the Wright brothers took off into history!

By Glen Phelan

A strong wind blew over Kitty Hawk, North Carolina. It chilled the air. It blew stinging sand across the beach. Even worse, it might make flying dangerous. Wilbur and Orville Wright hoped the wind would stop.

It didn't. So the two men took a chance. Orville got into the flying machine. He grabbed its controls. The engine rumbled. The plane started to move. Wilbur ran alongside to steady the wings. Then the plane lifted off the ground—and into history!

More than 100 years have passed since this flight. How did the Wright brothers become the first people to fly? This is their story.

Wilbur Wright, 13   **Orville Wright, 9**

Flying Toys

The Wright brothers became interested in flying as kids. In 1878, their father gave them a toy. The boys called it the Bat.

Wilbur and Orville studied how the Bat worked. They played with it until it broke. Then what did they do? Did they throw the Bat away? Not these kids.

They looked at how the toy was put together. Then they built a new one. Then another, and another. Each one was better.

That is how these boys were. They were curious. They wanted to know how things worked.

Wheels and Wings

When they got older, the brothers opened a bike shop. They sold and fixed bikes. They even built bikes of their own. But they never lost their dream of flying.

One day, they saw a photo of Otto Lilienthal. Otto flew **gliders.** A glider is a kind of plane. It has wings but it does not have an engine. Gliders can be hard to control. They rely on the wind.

Otto died in a glider crash. This showed Orville and Wilbur the dangers of flying. They still wanted to try. They planned to build a flying machine. But first, they had a lot to learn.

"The Flying Man." *That's what newspapers nicknamed Otto Lilienthal (right). The German engineer made 2,000 glider flights.*

Learning to Fly

Orville and Wilbur studied hard. They read books about flight. They wrote to experts.

They figured out that a flying machine needs three things:

1. It needs **wings** to lift itself into the air. The wings should be curved on top.

2. It needs a source of **power,** such as an engine.

3. It needs **controls** for steering.

Other people had already tested wings and engines. The biggest problem was the controls. Steering an aircraft was hard. A small wind could shake the wings. Then the machine might crash.

Bird Watching

The Wright brothers watched large birds called buzzards. These birds kept balanced by twisting the tips of their wings.

The brothers got an idea. Maybe they could twist, or **warp,** the wings of their plane. It just might work.

Buzzard

Big Day. *Orville Wright's diary (above) is open to December 17, 1903—the date of his historic flight.*

Flying Lessons. *Wilbur Wright pilots a glider in October 1902. This success encouraged the Wrights to build an engine-powered aircraft.*

Kites and Gliders

Wilbur and Orville tested their idea on a kite. They tied strings to the tips of the kite. They pulled the strings for control.

Next, the Wrights built a glider. Making a glider was not easy, though. It took two years to get the design right.

The Right Wings

The Wright brothers tested their first glider in 1900. It stayed in the air for only a short time.

So the Wright brothers got busy. They tried many different wings. They tested many shapes. At last, they found a design that worked. That was in August 1902.

Walking Tall. *Orville (at left) and Wilbur Wright visit a New York air show in 1910. By then the brothers were famous pilots.*

Making History

Would *Flyer 1* really fly? Orville and Wilbur were ready to find out. They took the plane to Kitty Hawk. But there were problems from the start. Storms kept them on the ground. Then the propellers broke. A month passed.

Finally, the brothers were ready. Wilbur was the first to try the plane. It started to lift into the air. But he pulled too hard on the controls. He crashed into the sand. Repairing the plane took two days.

Now it was Orville's turn. *Flyer 1* lifted up and stayed in the air! The flight lasted only 12 seconds. Yet it made history. *Flyer 1* became the world's first airplane.

Powered Flight

Now Wilbur and Orville were ready for the last big step. They added power. The Wright brothers built their own engine. The engine turned **propellers.** These pushed the plane through the air. Soon, the brothers had their first flying machine. They called it *Flyer 1.*

Wordwise

glider: machine that is like an airplane, but without an engine

propeller: spinning part that pushes a plane through the air

warp: to twist

Concept Check

1 How does Sylvia Earle feel about the ocean? How do you know?

2 Why do chameleons change color? Give three examples.

3 Is global warming a problem? Why or why not?

4 Who are the Wright brothers? Why are they famous?

5 List one thing you learned and one inference you made.